Write Better Sentences and Paragraphs

Level 6
English

Previously published as 40 Elaboration Activities That Take Writing from Bland to Brilliant!
Grades 5–8 by Scholastic Inc.

This edition published by Scholastic Education International (Singapore) Private Limited
A division of Scholastic Inc.

First edition 2013

ISBN 978-981-07-5263-7

C. Complete each sentence with a suitable abstract noun.

1. There are many people in developed countries who continue to live in _____ and are not able to make ends meet.

2. Dogs are known for their _____ and that's what makes them man's best friend.

3. The stray cat did not have anything to eat for days and finally died from _____.

4. Her _____ will not allow her to accept defeat so easily.

5. She was given a medal for her _____ during the disaster.

D. Complete each sentence. Use an abstract noun in each sentence.

1. She had never seen anything like that before so _____

_____.

2. The race was one of the closes in history and _____

_____.

3. The soldiers were not motivated by money; _____

_____.

4. _____

and wanted nothing more than to get rid of her rival.

5. We should view people based on merit _____.

Active Adjectives 1

Adjectives describe qualities of the nouns attached to them. When a few adjectives are used together, they follow a sequence:

Observation	Size	Shape	Age	Color	Origin	Material	Qualifier/Purpose	Noun
Expensive			antique			jade		vase
	big	round		green				shell
					American		Math	teacher

A. Complete the table with suitable adjectives for each category.

No.	Observation	Size	Shape	Age	Color	Origin	Material	Qualifier/Purpose	Noun
1.									apples
2.									books
3.									hut
4.									boy
5.									shoes

B. Read the sentences and fill in each blank with the most suitable adjectives.

1. Sally's fiancé bought her an _____ _____ ring for their wedding.

2. You need to wrap this _____ _____ bottle with paper to prevent it from breaking.

3. The _____ _____ boy looked at the big bully towering over him and felt his legs wobble like jelly.

4. Bella felt like a mermaid swimming in the _____

_____ sea.

5. My grandmother keeps her coins in _____ _____
_____ tins. Each tin still smells of butter, almond, and chocolate.

6. My brother bought a _____ _____

_____ car after he got his promotion.

C. Read the following journal. Fill in each blank with a suitable adjective to better describe a scary nightmare.

The (1) _____ wind howled through the

(2) _____ windows. I was standing at the bottom of a

long (3) _____ staircase. I wanted to run but I could not.

My (4) _____ legs just would not move. Pong, pong

pong! I turned and looked at the (5) _____ door. Who

could it be? Then I heard a hissing sound behind me. I turned and saw an

(6) _____ cobra staring menacingly at me. It had

(7) _____ eyes that monitored my every move.

What do I do?

Active Adjectives 2

We used **comparative** and **superlative adjectives** to compare nouns. We use comparative adjectives to compare two nouns and superlative adjectives to compare two or more nouns. We sometimes add *more* and *most* for two or more syllable adjectives.

A.   Complete the table below with the comparative and superlative adjectives.

Adjective	Comparative	Superlative
long		
noisy		
funny		
majestic		
complicated		
beautiful		
good		
bad		
many		

B.   Complete the sentences below with comparative and superlative adjectives.

1.   The young man was _____ (good) than his brother in many ways.

2.   Not only was he _____ (diligent), he was also _____ (intelligent).

14

3. Many also thought that he was one of the _____ (good-looking) men in the office.

4. He had a great sense of humor and was the _____ (funny) person around.

5. There wasn't much you could fault him for, except that he had one of the _____ (messy) desks in the office.

C. Fill in each blank with suitable adjectives to complete the description.

Walk along Banyan Avenue and look out for a (1) _____ white church on your left. Walk on till you reach a (2) _____ row of shops. This is the (3) _____ place in the neighborhood. You can hear all the buzzing even from a distance. The first salon has the (4) _____ service. The hairdresser never smiles. The last café serves the (5) _____ coffee. The lady boss is one of the (6) _____ people I've ever met and she remembers all her customers' names.

D. Think of three adjectives you can use to describe your favorite place. Write the superlative and comparative forms on the lines provided.

Adjective	Comparative	Superlative

Vivid Verbs 1

Verbs express action. **Vivid verbs** help bring the action to life.

Okay: Charlie <u>drinks</u> his tea quietly.

Better: Charlie <u>sips</u> his tea quietly.

A.   Complete the following tables with creative vivid verbs to engage your reader.

Vivid verbs for a bully	Vivid verbs for a hero	Vivid verbs for a timid girl
To look: _____ _____	To look: _____ _____	To look: _____ _____
To say: _____ _____	To say: _____ _____	To say: _____ _____
To move: _____ _____	To move: _____ _____	To move: _____ _____

B. Now, replace the underlined verbs in the sentences below with alternative verbs. Write two more vivid verbs on the lines.

1. Nurse Nancy <u>looked at</u> the patient.   _____ _____

2. The winner <u>walked</u> on stage to get his prize.   _____ _____

3. "Your handwriting is really ugly!" <u>said</u> Duncan.   _____ _____

4. The angry customer <u>came</u> into the shop.   _____ _____

5. After a long day, Miko <u>sat</u> on her sofa.   _____ _____

6. "She <u>forgot</u> to close the windows again," said Rani.   _____ _____

7. Tom <u>threw</u> his opponent out of the ring.   _____ _____

8. The two burglars <u>came</u> into the house.   _____ _____

C. Use some of the vivid verbs that you have listed above to write five sentences.

_____

_____

_____

_____

_____

Vivid Verbs 2

Vague dull verbs bog down writing and bore the reader. **Vivid verbs** add vigor and vitality to your writing.

Okay: The fans <u>talk</u> about their champion.

Better: The fans <u>boast</u> about their champion.

A.   Complete the following sentences with vivid verbs to illustrate the meaning in brackets.

1.   The boy _____ when he saw the thief robbing the woman.
            (shouted loudly)

2.   The horse _____ away into the forest.
            (ran quickly)

3.   The car _____ to a sudden halt.
            (in a loud, piercing cry)

4.   Benny _____ his food as he was starving!
            (ate quickly)

B.   Write three other more vivid verbs for each of the following verbs.

1.   Drink   _____ _____ _____

2.   Get   _____ _____ _____

3.   Think   _____ _____ _____

4.   Go   _____ _____ _____

C. Read the following passage. It is full of bland, lifeless verbs. Replace at least ten dull and overused verbs with vivid and more vibrant ones. Then rewrite the passage with your verbs below.

The giant looked around his garden. He saw some children playing around in it and he got mad. He wanted them out of his garden. So he shouted at them and told them to go away. The children looked at the enormous giant in fright and shivered in fear. They ran away as fast as their legs could carry them. The giant locked the gate to keep them out.

_____

_____

_____

_____

_____

_____

_____

_____

_____

Vivid Paragraphs

Remember **specific nouns** and **vivid verbs** help your reader visualize your story better. **Adjectives** make your nouns and pronouns clearer too.

A.   Fill in each blank with a suitable word from respective word lists.

radio	hurled	hot	scratches	steel
lifted	cold	body	suitcase	bruises

James had always been curious about Grandpa's (1) _____.

It was made of the strongest (2) _____ to withstand shock and

(3) _____. Once, James really (4) _____ it down the staircase

for a test and all it got were faint (5) _____ on the sides. No wonder

it was Grandpa's favorite traveling companion.

summer	legs	fracture	neat	fly
nest	leave	wings	winter	wound

Hannah watched as her friends disappeared into the horizon. She wished

she could (1) _____ with them to the south this year. Hannah tried

to move her (2) _____, but they still hurt. She would need weeks to

recover from her (3) _____. Hannah wept and cuddled up in her little

(4) _____. This would be the loneliest (5) _____ for the poor bird.

B. Replace each underlined word with a specific noun, vivid verb or suitable adjective to make the story better. Write your amended story on the lines below.

Dark clouds hovered and the wind began to <u>blow</u>. The tropical <u>rain</u> had finally come. The roof <u>shook</u> as the wind grew stronger and the rain <u>came</u> down on the farmhouse. Uncle Jim <u>ran</u> out to check on the animals. The <u>animals</u> were banging hard in the stable. Uncle Jim used all his might to <u>close</u> the old wooden gate. By the time he could shut it, the <u>frightened</u> animals had become <u>loud</u>. Uncle Jim ran around calming them down. Finally, he was so <u>tired</u> that he <u>sat</u> on the floor. It was a <u>bad</u> day that summer.

_____

_____

_____

_____

_____

_____

_____

_____

Adverbs 1

Adverbs modify verbs, adjectives and other adverbs. Adverbs answer questions like *how, when, where, how often, how many* or *how much.*

A. Answer the following questions as honestly as you can. Use suitable adverbs from the box in your answers.

daily	weekly	usually	always	seldom	before
after	a few	at least	better	well	best
more	earlier	slowly	loudly	gently	excitedly

1. How often do you play computer games?

    _____

2. Where do you normally go with your friends?

    _____

3. How much time do you spend watching TV each day?

    _____

4. At which place would you like to go for a yummy meal?

    _____

5. What do you wish your parents would say if you fail a test?

    _____

B. Complete the following journal entry with the most suitable adverb in the box.

quickly	loudly	gently	fondly	richly
brightly	quietly	slowly	excitedly	busily
eagerly	sadly	friendly	carefully	frantically

"Wake up, you sleepyhead," said Dad nudging me (1) _____ from my cozy bed. It was Aunt Nelly's wedding day and we had to be at Grandpa's home before 6 a.m. Thank goodness, Mum had woken up earlier and prepared breakfast. We gobbled it up (2) _____ and zoomed over in a flash.

Aunt May opened the door (3) _____ even before we could knock. Uncle Heng waved (4) _____ from behind. Most relatives had arrived. Grandma was still cooking (5) _____ in the kitchen. It was noisy everywhere but Grandpa sat (6) _____ at his favorite corner. As usual, we ran over and hugged Grandpa (7) _____. He smiled (8) _____, as always.

Suddenly, there was a loud honk outside. Uncle Heng grabbed two oranges and waited (9) _____ for the cue. Aunt May checked everything (10) _____ and waved her hand. It was time to welcome the bridegroom!

Adverbs 2

Adverbs answer questions like *how, when, where, how often, how many* or *how much.*

Vague: Should teachers allow calculators in math class?

Better: Should teachers <u>ever</u> allow calculators in math class?

A. Imagine that you have just got a new neighbor and you noticed something strange about him or her. Write adverbs to answer the following questions about him or her.

1. How would you describe the way your neighbor

   • walks   _____ _____

   • speaks   _____ _____

   • looks at you   _____ _____

2. Where does your neighbor usually

   • spend time   _____ _____

   • sit   _____ _____

3. When do you usually see your neighbor?   _____

4. What does your neighbor do that is unusual?

   _____

   _____

   _____

5.   How often does your neighbor do these unusual things?

_____

_____

B.   Use the information that you have listed in Part A to write a description about your strange new neighbor.

_____

_____

_____

_____

_____

_____

_____

_____

_____

_____

_____

Add Adjectives and Adverbs

Adjectives usually go before the word they modify. **Adverbs** can go before or after the word they modify. Using active adjectives and adverbs can make your writing come alive.

Okay: The protesters held up signs and shouted.

Better: The angry protesters held up signs and shouted.

The angry protesters held up signs and shouted indignantly.

A.   Complete the following beginnings with more details. You may use the adjectives and adverbs in the box.

smelly, old, skinny	young king puzzled	peered out nervously
loved to danced wildly	beautiful weather	stood their anxious
heard the thunder	not a single cloud	parents
rumbling	shouting hysterically	immediately leapt up
put on her best dress	giant octopus	fell into their loving arms

Long ago, deep in the forest of Enchanter Island...

All of a sudden, the ship rocked violently...

Finally, the door creaked open...

B. Make the paragraph better by adding adjectives and adverbs where appropriate. You may also want to replace some of the adjectives or adverbs in this paragraph.

The two brothers were close. In fact, they used to do everything together and they would tell each other everything. People used to comment that they were always happy when they were together. Everything changed after the misunderstanding they had. Keegan thought that Kane had prevented him from getting into the football team by telling the coach about a previous injury. The injury was not serious but it was enough to make the coach choose another student. Keegan was angry and he felt betrayed.

_____

_____

_____

_____

_____

_____

_____

_____

_____

_____

Synonyms

> **Synonyms** are words that have similar meanings. However, not all synonyms for a word are that close in meaning. Synonyms for a word are synonymous with one another. For example, *nibble* and *gorge* are both synonyms for *eat*, but not for each other.

A. Complete the following table by listing two synonyms of the word in the preceding column. You may want to use a thesaurus to help you. The first one has been done for you.

Eat	Nibble	Peck
		Gnaw
	Gorge	Gobble
		Devour

Speak		

Shout		

Like		

B. Replace the underlined words with synonyms to create a more intense image. Write the revised paragraph below.

Marilyn was <u>worried</u> about the performance. She looked out and saw the <u>people</u> and the <u>bright</u> stage lights. It would be her first time performing in front of such a <u>large</u> audience. She wanted to <u>shout</u> to relieve the stress she felt. Then she heard the host <u>say</u> her name. It was time for her to <u>go</u> on stage. She <u>hoped</u> that she would remember all her lines. It has always been her <u>wish</u> to be an actress and here she was – <u>acting</u> in her first ever play. She must do <u>well</u>. She walked <u>calmly</u> onto the stage and played her part <u>wonderfully</u>. The <u>loud</u> applause she <u>got</u> surprised her. She was so <u>happy</u> that she wanted to <u>jump</u> for joy on stage!

_____

_____

_____

_____

_____

_____

_____

_____

_____

_____

To parents Choose an excerpt from a book and challenge your child to improve the story by replacing verbs, adjectives, and adverbs with more intense synonyms.

Date: _____

Alternate with Antonyms

Antonyms are words that are opposite in meaning. They can create an opposing point of view in your story. The second sentence creates an opposing joyful mood about the place.

Negative: The <u>kindergarten</u> was buzzing with <u>shouting teachers</u>.

Positive: The <u>kindergarten</u> was buzzing with <u>giggling kids</u>.

A. In each sentence, circle the word that can be replaced with an antonym from the box to create an opposing point of view. Write the word on the line.

boring   sobbed   hero   children   bright   receive

1. The villain sailed away in the boat. _____

2. This is the most hilarious joke I have ever heard! _____

3. Make sure the forgetful elderly return all the tools. _____

4. Evelyn laughed till tears rolled down her cheeks. _____

5. The room was so dark that I could not sleep. _____

6. The children give presents every Christmas. _____

B. Read the following paragraphs. Circle the words you can change to show an opposing point of view and replace each with an antonym.

Paragraph 1

Mum never understands me. She nags at my dirty nails and horrible handwriting. That's style, you know. I try to be neat, but I just can't. I hate broccoli. My nightmare! And Mum's is the worst. Once, I failed my test and she screamed and even cried.

_____

_____

_____

_____

Paragraph 2

The Tinker clan was the largest tribe in the jungle. The women always frowned and were very rowdy. The men were similar. They were the most reserved people on earth rejecting us with waving knives and cheers every time we were near their palaces.

_____

_____

_____

_____

Funny Antonyms

> Sometimes, writers use **antonyms** to create humor, irony or sarcasm.
>
> *Description:*   The soup was as delicious as stale broth!
>
> *Meaning:*   The soup tasted horrible.

A.   Replace the underlined word in each phrase with an antonym.

1.	a <u>safe</u> investment	
2.	<u>reduce</u> soreness	
3.	an <u>amateur</u> car repair job	
4.		as <u>clumsy</u> as ever
5.	see you at the <u>summit</u>	
6.		as a <u>punishment</u>
7.		the most <u>ridiculous</u> reply
8.		the <u>fatigue</u> was overwhelming
9.	the <u>first</u> team	
10.		sleeps like a <u>baby</u>

B.   Complete the following sentences with above phrases to create sarcasm.

1.   Putting your money with that conman has to be _____ if you've got loads of money to lose.

2.   "I'll _____," mocked Chris as he continued climbing.

3.   "_____," said Gina sorely, "I could feel the enthusiasm of the crowd!"

4.   If that was supposed to be an answer to my question, it must be

_____ I'd ever heard.

5. _____ for your actions, you will get five hours of detention after class today!

C. Use some of the phrases above to write ironic sentences.

_____

_____

_____

_____

_____

_____

D. Complete the sentences using antonyms to create humor.

1. His classmates like to tease him by calling him _____ even though he was one of the tallest boys in class.

2. She was so angry with him that she couldn't _____ at him and just stared at him with her mouth open.

3. "Thanks for the _____ present," said Carol weakly as she looked miserably at the ugly sweater she got for Christmas!

4. "Be _____ is not exactly something you would say to someone who is sad," said Jim as he rolled his eyes at Tina.

To parents Ask your child to read some of the sentences above and think about the tone of voice that would be used in those instances.

33

Supporting Details

An idea without support is vague. Even a sentence that is technically correct can be unclear. You can improve your writing by adding clear, vivid details to strengthen an idea.

A. Look at the topic sentence below. Some details have been provided. Think of other details that might support the topic sentence. Use the questions provided.

TOPIC: Swimming is very beneficial to health.

SUPPORTING DETAILS:

- Works all the muscles in the body

- Develops strength, cardiovascular fitness

- Does not cause some of the injuries that can be sustained from high-impact activities

- _____ (How does it impact mental health?)

- _____ (How does it help with weight loss?)

B. Now use the topic sentence and the supporting points to write a short paragraph on the topic.

_____

_____

_____

C. Write on a topic related to healthy living. Write the goal in the center and use the web to gather supporting details for your idea.

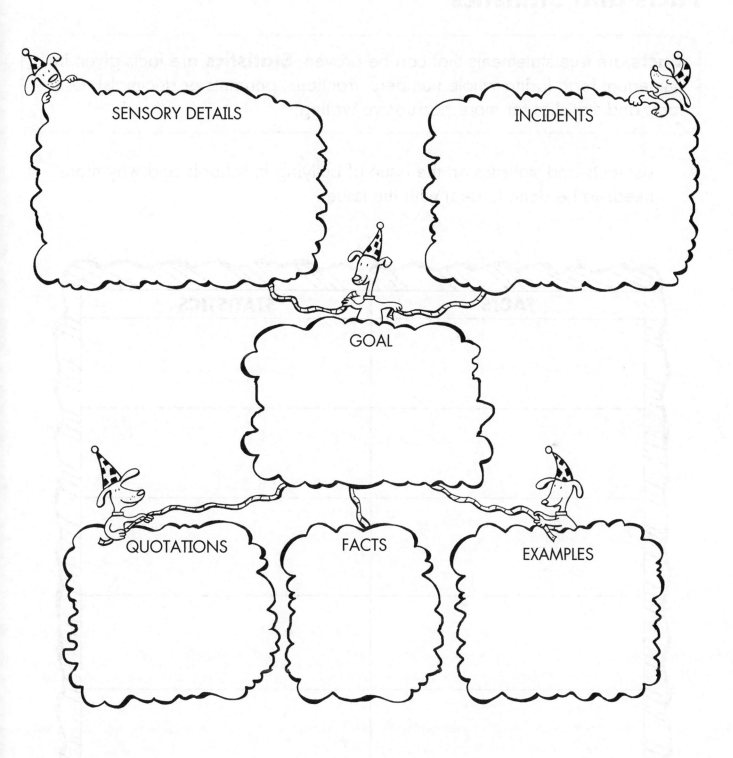

SENSORY DETAILS

INCIDENTS

GOAL

QUOTATIONS

FACTS

EXAMPLES

To parents Get your child to write a paragraph using the points in the graphic organizer in Part C.

35

Facts and Statistics

> **Facts** are true statements that can be proven. **Statistics** are facts given in numerical form (using whole numbers, fractions, percents or decimals). Use facts and statistics for more persuasive writing.

A. List facts and statistics on the issue of bullying in schools and why more needs to be done to deal with the issue.

FACTS	STATISTICS

B. Plan and write a persuasive paragraph on your view, using the facts and statistics from Part A.

Beginning topic sentence	_____ _____ _____ _____
Supporting facts and statistics	_____ _____ _____ _____ _____ _____ _____ _____ _____
Ending statement	_____ _____ _____ _____

Supporting Examples

One way to add detail is to give examples that support the main idea. Good examples help readers to make connections. When you write it is important to think about how someone else may find loopholes in your argument if you do not have good supporting examples.

A. Think about the topic: Regular visits to the dentist are essential. Write two topic sentences and include two examples to support and refute each topic sentence.

Topic Sentence	Examples to Support	Examples to Refute

Topic Sentence	Examples to Support	Examples to Refute

B. Choose one topic sentence. Write a paragraph to support the topic.

_____

_____

C. Now write a paragraph to refute the other topic statement. Use the examples you have listed to refute the argument.

_____

_____

_____

_____

_____

D. Now rewrite the paragraph in Part B. Use both the examples listed in Part A to refute the argument.

For example: *There have been many improvements in toothbrushes so normal brushing is able to remove a lot of plaque from our teeth.*

_____

_____

_____

_____

_____

Debating the Issue

When writing to discuss an issue, it is important to present both sides of an argument before coming to a conclusion. This would make your argument more credible as it would have considered the pros and cons instead of being a one-sided point of view.

A. Imagine you are writing an article for your school magazine. Fill in your ideas in the graphic organizer.

Topic: Schools should have nap time for students

Benefits	Problems
Benefit 1: Supporting examples:	Problem 1: Supporting examples:
Benefit 2: Supporting examples:	Problem 2: Supporting examples:

B.   With the ideas in Part A, write a short passage for your school magazine.

INTRODUCTION: (Topic, main ideas to consider)
MAIN IDEA 1: (Elaborate on benefits)
MAIN IDEA 2: (Elaborate on problems)
CONCLUSION: (Either a summary of the main ideas or state your opinion)

Cause and Effect

Everything that happens can affect the whole situation. When you identify the **cause and effect**, you allow your readers to see one event affects another.

A.   Fill in each blank with an answer from the box. Write C for 'Cause' or E for 'Effect' beside your answer.

because Wolly forgot to turn off the tap   and you will get a free mug
when the celebrity soccer player arrived   the mountaineers could see the peak
the sniper aimed at the target   after a long day out at sea
having run 5km round the field   Jane was scolded

1.   The bathroom was flooded _____. (_____)

2.   The class cheered _____. (_____)

3.   Bumping into Mum, _____. (_____)

4.   As the sun rose, _____. (_____)

5.   The fishermen loaded their catch onto the jetty _____

     _____. (_____)

6.   Buy two sacks of rice _____. (_____)

7.   Patrick huffed and puffed _____. (_____)

8.   At the command, _____. (_____)

B. Combine the two sentences into one sentence to show the cause and effect. Remember to use the correct connectors in your sentences.

1. It was snowing outside. School was closed for the day.

   _____

2. She missed the bus. She woke up late.

   _____

3. Keane left home in a hurry. He left the report he had been working on at home.

   _____

4. He failed to pay his taxes. He had to pay a hefty fine.

   _____

5. The manager was promoted. He came up with a way to save money for the company.

   _____

C. Complete each sentence starter and write what happens as a result of the action in the first part of the sentence.

1. Due to the heavy snowfall, _____.

2. The slippery roads caused _____.

3. As the roads were inaccessible to traffic, _____.

4. Since we could not get out of the house, _____.

To parents Ask your child to write three more cause and effect sentences to continue the story in Part C.

Drawing Comparisons

Sometimes, writers **draw comparisons** with famous characters to help the reader understand a particular character. It assumes that the reader would also be familiar with that character.

A. Read this adapted classic story of *Snow White* written by Brothers Grimm.

Jealousy was indeed a green monster. The Queen mother's scheme had worked. Snow White, as pure as a dove, had truly believed her. Without a doubt, Snow White took a big bite of the apple and sank into deep sleep. Like bees, the dwarves scuttled about trying to wake Snow White up. Suddenly, the galloping of a horse broke through the silence of the forest. The dwarves peeked from the bushes. In a distance, was a prince in shiny armor. Hope had come!

B. Complete each sentence with the best comparison. Write the letter of the correct answer in the bracket.

1. "Jerry must lose this time!" Gina smirked like the _____ setting up the trap for Snow White.

   (a) dwarves
   (b) evil Queen Mother
   (c) Prince   (   )

2. "Are you _____? How can you be so naïve?"

   (a) dwarf
   (b) Snow White
   (c) Prince   (   )

3. Like _____, he rescued the pretty girl from the gangsters.

   (a) one of the seven dwarves
   (b) Snow White's stepmother
   (c) a prince in shiny armor   (   )

44

C. Think of some famous people or characters you know. Write down three characteristics they are known for. The first one has been done for you.

1. Mother Teresa   <u>Self-sacrificing, lives in poverty, looks after the sick</u>

2. _____   _____

3. _____   _____

4. _____   _____

5. _____   _____

6. _____   _____

D. Write descriptions of people alluding to the famous people or characters above. Remember to use their characteristics. The first one has been done for you.

1. She was the Mother Teresa in the village as she sacrificed all her time looking after those in need.

2. _____

_____

3. _____

_____

4. _____

_____

Similes

> A **simile** compares two things. Some similes compare two things using the word *like* or the structure *as* _____ *as*.

A. Read the following story. Fill in each blank with the correct simile from the box.

like a mad dog	as cool as a cucumber
like a baby	as quick as lightning
like a bull	as happy as a lark
like a cheese bun	as stubborn as a donkey

I really don't know what was wrong with my sister. One moment, she was

(1) _____, giggling at my jokes. The next moment,

she snapped at me (2) _____ yapping away. She

even charged at me (3) _____. I really thought

she was going to knock me over. (4) _____,

I ducked and she banged right into the cupboard. Immediately, her forehead

swelled up (5) _____. She wailed at the top

of her voice. I didn't know what to do. Mum was the best. She was

(6) _____. Without a word, Mum simple cuddled

my sister who was sobbing (7) _____. I think that

my sister was simply acting up to get some attention. I would like to give her a

pep talk but it would be useless. She never listens to anyone. She is

(8) _____.

B.   Complete each sentence with an appropriate simile of your own.

1.   You stink like _____. Go and take your shower now!

2.   I feel happy seeing Janice because her smile is always _____.

3.   Dad should stop visiting the casino. Gambling is like _____.

4.   Grandpa is _____ whenever he loses his reading glasses.

C.   The following are some common similes. Use them to complete the sentences.

as proud as a peacock	as plain as day	as slow as a snail
like silk	as solid as a rock	as timid as a rabbit
like a giraffe	as stubborn as a mule	

1.   A baby's skin is free from any blemish and smooth _____.

2.   He can be a basketball player since he is tall _____.

3.   She is _____ and is always the last person to reach.

4.   That girl was _____ and thought that everyone else was beneath her.

5.   The cowardly boy is _____.

6.   He is so reliable; he is _____.

7.   It is very obvious who did it; the answer is _____.

8.   You are _____ and won't listen to anyone's advice.

Metaphors

A **metaphor** compares two things that seem unrelated. A metaphor gets readers to understand or experience one idea in terms of another in fresh or interesting ways.

A. Read each metaphor. Identify what is being compared by completing the equation. Then explain the meaning of the metaphor in your own words.

1. Reading on a rainy day is heaven to me _____ = _____

   Meaning: _____

2. When Darren tore my project, I turned into a volcano and gave him a punch. _____ = _____

   Meaning: _____

3. The small boy is a little prince at home. _____ = _____

   Meaning: _____

4. He has a heart of stone and nothing can move him. _____ = _____

   Meaning: _____

5. She is a walking dictionary and has a wide range of vocabulary. _____ = _____

   Meaning: _____

B. Read the following story. Fill in each blank with the correct word from the box.

mouse	hero	fox	bulls
ostrich	fool	giant	rag doll

"Stop being an (1) _____ and trying to bury your head in

a hole!" screamed Ronney tugging at Marc's collar. Everyone watched as

Marc was flung about in the air. He was a (2) _____ in Ronney's

(3) _____ hands. It was terrible to watch, but I would

be a (4) _____ to stop Ronney now.

Just then, the (5) _____ arrived. Mr Stephen appeared at the door.

"Stop right there. What is all this about?" said Mr Stephen pulling the two

hotheaded (6) _____ apart. "Marc is a real (7) _____!

We want him to tell you the truth!" cried Ronney. "What truth?" asked

Mr Stephen turning to look at Marc who had become a (8) _____.

"I..I...was the one who stole the missing specimen," Marc stammered.

Personification

> **Personification** is a kind of metaphor. When writers use personification, they give human qualities or abilities to nonhuman things or ideas.
>
> *Example:*   Shadows dance across the floor.
>
> *Personification:* Shadows can not really dance; people can dance.
>
> *Meaning:*   Shadows move rhythmically or gracefully, as if they had legs and really could dance.

A.   Read each example of personification. Explain its meaning in your own words.

1.   The flames mocked the rescue workers.

      Meaning: _____

2.   The sun tiptoed into my dream.

      Meaning: _____

3.   The engine groaned as we drove away.

      Meaning: _____

4.   The trees bowed on either side of the path.

      Meaning: _____

5.   My laptop threw a fit when I tried to use it and then died on me.

      Meaning: _____

6.   The heavy old wooden door protested loudly as I shoved it open.

      Meaning: _____

B. Choose an inanimate (nonliving) object from the first box. Personify it with one of the characteristics or traits from the second box.

| waves   flowers   stars | danced   winked   lashed |

_____

_____

_____

_____

_____

C. Choose an inanimate (nonliving) object from the first box. Personify it with one characteristics or traits of one of the people in the second box.

| bus   sunset   volcano | artist   chef   soldier   waiter |

1. _____

2. _____

3. _____

Anthropomorphic Characters

When your animal or plant characters have human characteristics, they are called **anthropomorphic characters**. For example:

Just as the lion was dozing off, something ran up his tail, onto his back and stood on his head. Irritated, the lion swatted hard and a mouse dropped right before him. "How dare you disturb my sleep?" roared the lion. "Please let me go, Your Majesty! I promised to be your friend forever. I will save you if you were in trouble," pleaded the mouse shaking.

Adapted from *The Lion and The Mouse* in *Aesop's Fables*

In the above story, the lion was a king while the mouse tried to be a friend.

A.   Complete the graphic organizer for two characters from the story *No More Lies*.

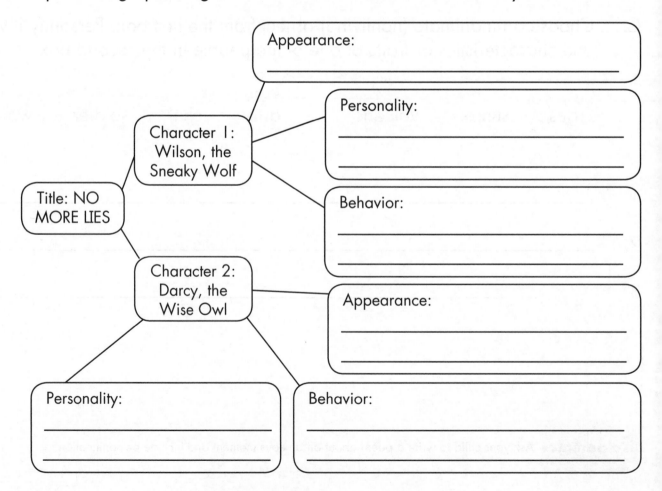

B. With the ideas in Part A, write a short story of *No More Lies* in the space below.

_____

_____

_____

_____

_____

_____

_____

_____

_____

_____

_____

_____

Accenting with Figurative Language

Whenever you describe something by comparing it with something else without using the actual meaning of the words, you are using **figurative language**. For example, using simile, metaphor, personification etc. in your writing.

A.   Fill in the blanks with the best answer in the box.

a bank	like soldiers	as hot as an oven	a tortoise
like vultures	danced beautifully	as smooth as glass	hell
a chicken	flashed		

1.   Once the supermarket opened, Mandy and Dan went straight for the food

section _____.

2.   You must try this lotion. It will make your skin _____.

3.   Have you forgotten to switch on the air-conditioner? The room is

_____.

4.   The bottles are lined neatly in a row _____.

5.   It is _____ living here with neighbors shouting at one another all day long.

6.   Jasmine was _____ hiding under the table during jab time.

7.   That spoilt rich boy thinks his father is _____ and always asks him for money.

8.   Sam takes his time to do everything. He is really _____.

9. The lighthouse _____ his beams right out across the ocean.

10. The trees _____ in the autumn wind. Soon, they would be bald.

B. Plan a description of a character. What qualities does your character have?

_____

_____

_____

_____

_____

C. Now think of associations for your character. Does your character have qualities similar to an animal, another famous character or an object? List four different things that it could be.

_____

_____

_____

_____

_____

Imagery

A good story paints pictures in the reader's mind. It engages the senses of the readers, so that he can experience the story with the characters.

A. Read the pairs of sentences. Which is better? Underline the better sentence.

(A1) The class was boring.

(A2) The class yawned at the droning of the teacher.

(B1) Bob is a good boy.

(B2) Wiping off the tears on his mother's cheeks, Bob whispered, "Don't worry, Mum. Dad will get well soon."

(C1) The performance was great.

(C2) The audience rose and gave thunderous applause.

(D1) The storm was bad.

(D2) The howling of the wind grew louder with each clap of thunder. The roof rattled as the bulb swung about wildy.

B. Choose the best word for the situation. Write the letter of your answer in the blank space.

1. Everyone _____ the moment Benny entered. He was the tyrant of the class!

(a) stopped   (b) froze   (c) thickened

2. The _____ of the siren broke the silence of the night. Another murder again.

(a) screaming   (b) screeching   (c) stammering

3. Tears fell as Rina rubbed her swollen cheeks. Sarah had never _____ her till now.

(a) strangled   (b) slapped   (c) kicked

C. List phrases or words related to the following emotions.

Situation	See	Smell	Taste	Touch	Hear
Joy					
Anger					
Sadness					

D. Make this story more vivid to the readers. Fill in each blank with the best answer from the box.

said	burst	screamed	broke
black	stink	ploughed	choking

Boom! The ground trembled and a car (1) _____ into flames.

A crowd gathered as (2) _____ smoke covered the afternoon

sun. Like a crazy woman, Wendy (3) _____ through the crowd.

"No no," cried the young mother. The air was (4) _____ by now.

"Save my daughter!" (5) _____ Wendy.

To parents Have your child continue the story above with vivid descriptions of the scene.

Body Language 1

> You can show how your characters feel through their actions.
>
> *Okay:* The old lady was sad and lonely.
>
> *Better:* The old lady looked around at the empty house and stared blankly into space.

A. How does the character in each of these situations feel? Underline the body language the character displays which tells you so.

1. At the news, Mrs Jenny slumped and sobbed bitterly.

Feelings: _____

2. Amy pinched her cheeks hard. It's not a dream. She had really won a million dollars!

Feelings: _____

3. "You will be okay," assured Uncle John as he gave Tim a big hug.

Feelings: _____

4. "This is garbage," said Chef Daniel dumping the dish away.

Feelings: _____

5. Like a little girl, Jane danced around when she knew her dad had survived the surgery.

Feelings: _____

6. Jim crossed arms and glared at Tom. He was waiting for an apology.

Feelings: _____

B. Read the following note and write a story on how Marc overcame the problem and got his family back to the future. You may use the words in the box to make your story more interesting.

Marc has just discovered the secret code to the time machine. It could take his family back to the future. The only problem was that the Monkey clan had captured his family.

skipped with joy	hid the code	light went out
clambered through the window	fell with a thud	froze in fear
moonlight shining in	spotted Mom at a corner	scurried over
bit through the ropes	dashed for the time machine	

_____

_____

_____

_____

_____

_____

_____

_____

To parents Get your child to look at various pictures and describe the action of the person in the picture and the emotion that the person displays.

Body Language 2

> Showing how your characters feel through their actions might be a more effective way of getting your reader engaged than simply stating the emotion.

A. Think about the each of the following emotions. What kind of actions may a character experiencing these emotions display? Complete the table with phrases from the box. Then add your own examples.

Crossing of arms   Crossing fingers

Looking down   Pacing up and down

Punching the air   Slumping in the seat

Head in her hands   Skipping across the hall

Emotion	Actions
Sadness	
Anger	
Happy	
Nervous	
Victorious	

B.   Use the actions in Part A to write two paragraphs. Write a paragraph about:

1.   A character who is nervous about doing something for the first time but felt happy to have accomplished it.

_____

_____

_____

_____

_____

_____

2.   A character who is angry about being betrayed and sad because her friend betrayed her.

_____

_____

_____

_____

_____

_____

Collocations 1

A **collocation** is two or more words that often go together. These word combinations just sound "right" to English speakers, who use them all the time. On the other hand, other combinations may be unnatural and just sound "wrong". Having the right word collocations will make your writing sound more natural and easily understood.

A.   Match the right word to the sentence by writing correct letter.

a) business   b) bus   c) visit   d) down   e) battle
f) sack   g) away   h) care   i) bill   j) act

1.   The other team is just too strong. We are fighting a losing _____.

2.   Who is going to foot the _____ for this dinner?

3.   James was caught in the _____ when the police arrived.

4.   Let's get down to _____ and discuss the program for the graduation concert.

5.   Shall we pay Grandma a _____ since we are in town?

6.   Aunt Mary looked after her garden with tender loving _____.

7.   I need to catch the _____ or I will be late for the meeting.

8.   Charlie got the _____ for stealing the company computers.

9.   Please take _____ the message for me.

10.   What did you take _____ from the lecture today?

B.   Complete the sentences with the correct collocation from the box.

did her hair	broke the record	broke her promise
take a look	caught his attention	made a mess
went blind	came into view	save time
burst into tears	excruciating pain	completely satisfied

1.   Before the ball, my mother put on her make up and _____.

2.   She _____ with rage and nobody could make her see reason.

3.   The boy was in _____ after he fell and broke his leg.

4.   She _____ to her kids and did not bring them to the park.

5.   The lady was _____ with the service she got and gave the waiter a big tip.

6.   Please _____ outside and tell me if you see anything odd.

7.   The racer _____ for the world's fastest lap.

8.   The kids _____ of the place and left their mother to clean up after them.

9.   In order to _____, she skipped a few steps of the process.

10.   After I turned the corner, the building finally _____.

11.   The girl was so sad that she _____.

12.   The beautiful girl _____ and the prince could not take his eyes off her.

Collocations 2

A.   Complete the following table to make correct collocations. Words can be used more than once.

a difference	a good time	lunch	business
a compliment	the housework	a seat	interest
a cold	an exam	space	someone's life
fire	the law	a habit	trouble
a diary	the price	abroad	calm
clean	astray	a job	early

HAVE	DO	MAKE
TAKE	BREAK	CATCH
PAY	SAVE	KEEP
COME	GO	GET

B. Choose five of the collocations from the table and write a sentence using each collocation.

_____

_____

_____

_____

_____

_____

_____

_____

C. Read the following story and fill in each blank with the correct collocation.

have my fill	found a job	running out of cash
take a break	have a good time	grew dark

This was the first family vacation for Gary since Dad (1) _____

again. "We're going to (2) _____!" Gary squealed in delight.

They went on ride after ride in the theme park. Only when the sky

(3) _____ did they stop. "Let's (4) _____," said

Mum heading for the Japanese restaurant. "Hurray, I'm going to

(5) _____," said Gary. It was the best dinner ever. At the

cashier's, Dad frowned. "I'm (6) _____. Do you accept credit

card?" asked Dad. The cashier nodded.

Run-on Sentences

A **run-on sentence** is a sentence that runs into another sentence. The clauses in a run-on sentence are not properly connected and can be separated. Having too many run-on sentences in your writing will make it very hard to read.

A.   Correct the following run-on sentences. You can either break up the sentence into two sentences or add a suitable connector.

1.   Gary had a BBQ there were chicken, corn, and stingray.

_____

2.   Jean sketched the scenery Sally painted the sky and Polly added the borders.

_____

_____

3.   Like a bull Kim charged into the store he broke the glasses he kicked the cashier and snatched away the cash in the register.

_____

_____

4.   Have you ever seen a panda you must visit the zoo this autumn two pandas from China have arrived.

_____

_____

B. Correct the run-on sentences in the paragraph. Write your revised paragraph below.

Everyone wanted to know who the guilty party was and they all suspected it was Gerald he was always loitering around the locker area also he kept avoiding everyone. He must be the one who stole all the wallets during break time during assembly. They decided to follow him find out they saw him putting a letter into Lily's locker every day he did the same thing. Then Lily realized that her secret admirer was Gerald he had been giving her presents and love notes for weeks.

_____

_____

_____

_____

_____

_____

_____

_____

_____

_____

Cut the Clutter

It is important to write clearly and concisely. It is important to cut out unnecessary and repetitive words that do not add meaning to your sentence.

A.   Underline the redundant word(s) in each sentence.

1.   The tired and exhausted boys dragged huffed and puffed after running around the field for an hour.

2.   How Doris could spend all her money on that expensive costly dress?

3.   The famous Statue of Liberty is a well-known landmark in New York.

4.   Marcus stammered, stuttered and shivered every time the bully came near.

5.   The generous and giving driver always shared his food with the orphans.

6.   Barney was so clumsy that he fell into the sweet honey pot.

7.   Out in the rain, the scouts were drenched wet without a shelter in sight.

8.   Have you ever seen Bryan training so long and for so many hours in the boxing ring?

9.   She was one of the most important of the business people I had to meet.

10.   That professor could not have said it better than that.

11.   Living the high life has always been a dream of his that he has been wishing for since he was a young boy.

12.   He was such a proud, snobbish, and conceited person that no one could stand him.

B. Circle the redundant words in the following story. Then write the edited story in the lines below.

The Great Wall of China is one of the seven wonders in the whole wide world. It could even be seen and spotted from outer space. The Great Wall of China took many years and generations to be completed. It was used as a defense against invaders and enemies to keep them out of the country. The tyrant emperor made young and old men work in harsh conditions. Many perished and died while working on the wall. They never got home. It is one of the major achievements that the emperor Qin Shi Huang is known for.

_____

_____

_____

_____

_____

_____

_____

_____

_____

_____

_____

_____

Active and Passive Voice

When the subject does the action, the sentence is in **active voice**. When the subject receives the action, the sentence is in **passive voice**. We often use the passive voice when the action is more important or if the subject is not important.

Active: Larry punched Jack in the stomach.

Passive: Jack was punched in the stomach (by Larry).

A.   Are the following sentences in the active or passive voice? Write active or passive on the line. Then change the sentence to the other voice.

1.	At a wave of the wand, Wizard Warner turned Harry into a hawk. (_____)
2.	All the houses were swept into the sea during the hurricane. (_____)
3.	The durian fruit is considered a delicacy by some people. (_____)
4.	The police had warned the hooligans to stop extorting money from the boys. (_____)
5.	The drought killed many children in the village. (_____)

B. Read the story. Some sentences can be changed into another voice. Change them and write the revised story on the lines below.

Mandy looked up into the sky. The vultures had circled her for hours. Mandy huddled among the rocks. She had been exhausted from the battle. The gashing cut was widened by the constant running. The smell of fresh blood attracted the hungry vultures. The giant birds' cawing frightened Mandy, but she could run no more. She knew soon, the vultures would come swooping down.

_____

_____

_____

_____

_____

C. Write a paragraph using a mixture of active and passive voice. Use the points listed below. Decide which points focus on the action and would be more suitable for the passive voice.

the police conducted a search   helicopters used
the search lasted three days   entire area searched
found Mandy

_____

_____

_____

_____

Vary Sentence Structures 1

Variety is the splice of life. This applies to your writing as well. Good writers alternate sentence structures for variety. Here are three kinds of sentence structures:

- A **simple sentence** has one main clause, with one subject and one verb.

- A **compound sentence** has two or main clauses, usually linked with *and, or* or *but.*

- A **complex sentence** has one main clause and one or more subordinate clauses.

A. Identify each sentence by its structure.

1. The ptarmigan is a unique bird. _____

2. Although it is white in winter, it changes color in spring. _____

3. Color can be a good camouflage, but it won't always

   protect an animal. _____

4. Stick insects look like branches, which helps them get food. _____

5. There are many animals that use camouflage. _____

6. Some use them to catch prey and others use them to

   hide from danger. _____

B. Read the following simple sentences. Combine these sentences to construct compound or complex sentences. Then write a paragraph using a combination of all types of sentences.

Leonardo da Vinci was an Italian renaissance artist.
He was also known to be a sculptor, architect, mathematician, engineer and inventor.
The *Mona Lisa* is one of his famous paintings.
His other famous paintings include *The Last Supper*.
He was also revered for being an engineering genius.
He came up with the concepts for a helicopter, tank and even a calculator.
His journals often contained drawings of various inventions.
His also recorded his observations of anatomy in his journals.

_____

_____

_____

_____

_____

_____

_____

_____

Vary Sentence Structures 2

A. Choose a topic and come up with ten points you can think of about that
topic. You may use one of the following topics if you wish:

- A school trip
- A famous musician
- An argument with a friend
- Dangerous animals

_____

_____

_____

_____

_____

_____

_____

_____

_____

_____

B. Use the points you have come up with and write two sentences of each type.

Simple sentences:

_____

_____

_____

Compound sentences:

_____

_____

_____

Complex sentences:

_____

_____

_____

_____

The Voice

Having a clear writer's **voice** will engage your readers. To have a clear writer's voice, you have to:
- know who your readers are
- what your writing is for – to persuade, to inform or to entertain

You can create a clear writer's voice through good vocabulary, correct punctuation and good paragraphing.

A.   Read the following paragraph.

As you reach puberty, you may experience changes in your bodies. For boys, you may suddenly grow taller at an amazing speed of one to two centimeters a year. Your voice may break. Facial hair will start to appear around your lips and sides of your face. For the girls, you may experience bodily changes at least two years earlier than the boys. You will grow taller an average of about one centimeter a year.

Answer the following questions.

I.   Who do you think is the target reader? What makes you think so?

_____

_____

2.   What is the purpose of the writing?

_____

_____

3.   How has the writer made the paragraph appropriate for the reader?

_____

_____

B. Imagine that you need to write a short paragraph to encourage your friends to join your sports / activities club. Jot down about five points about your club.

_____

_____

_____

_____

_____

C. Use the points you have listed above to write a short text about your club. Remember who your target audience is and what the purpose of the text is.

_____

_____

_____

_____

_____

_____

_____

Biography and Autobiography

Biographies and **autobiographies** are accounts of a person's life. However, in biographies, the main character is different from the storyteller whereas in autobiographies, the main character of the life story is the same person who is telling the story.

A. Think about an incident that had a big impact on your life. Answer the following questions.

1. What happened in that incident?

_____

_____

_____

2. How did you feel?

_____

_____

_____

3. How did it impact your life and change you as a person?

_____

_____

_____

B.   Fill in the following graphic organizer with details of a famous person.

Name: _____

Early life:	
Important events in that person's life:	How the events shaped the person:
Major achievements:	How these achievements changed the world:
What you admire about that person:	

C.   Now, on a separate sheet of paper write a short biographical paragraph of this person.

To parents   Ask your child to look at the two pieces of writing in this unit and identify the main difference between the autobiography and biography.

Writing a List

Lists can be very useful. A list can help you achieve something or keep a record of things. A list can help to make your writing concise and easy to read. For example, *This project aims to*

- *show the life cycle of the fruit trees, and*
- *show the importance of insects in cross-pollination*

A. Imagine that you are going to write an essay about pollution (you may choose to focus on a particular type of pollution). List two main points that you would like to make in your essay.

1. _____

2. _____

B. Now, write the beginning of your essay on pollution. Include the two main points in the list as part of your introduction.

_____

_____

_____

_____

_____

_____

To parents Ask your child to think of other ways in which the above introduction might be written.

Setting the Tone

> The **tone** of a piece of writing is the **mood**. A text may be sarcastic, mysterious, dark or light-hearted and so on.

A.   Look at the words in the list. Group them under the correct category.

mournful	optimistic	relaxed	cheerful
quiet	skeptical	aloof	intimidating
comforting	irritated	bored	encouraging

POSITIVE TONE	NEUTRAL TONE	NEGATIVE TONE

B.   Read the following story. What tone or mood is it? How do your know?

First Day at School

The day Farah had been waiting for was finally here. Farah had long woken up before sunrise and washed up quickly. She looked at the blue pinafore in the wardrobe and beamed. "This is the most beautiful uniform I've ever seen," said Farah. Like a big girl, Farah put on the uniform and shoes. "Mum, Dad, hurry!" said Farah pounding on her parent's bedroom door.

Imagine Farah was anxious about going to school. Show how you would change the tone and mood in the lines below. You may use some of the words from the above story.

_____

_____

_____

_____

_____

_____

_____

_____

_____

_____

_____

_____

Story Planner

A good writer plans his story before writing the draft. A **story plan** helps the writer to think over and organize the ideas carefully. It includes SETTING, CHARACTER, PLOT, and CONCLUSION.

A. Think about your favorite story. How do you think the writer planned his story? Complete the graphic organizer below.

Story Title: _____

SETTING		
CHARACTERS		
Main Heroes	Main Villains	Other Characters

PLOT		
Introduction	Conflict	Resolution

CONCLUSION

To parents Ask your child to change some of the components of the story and rewrite the story with their changes.

B.   Imagine you are writing the following story. Plan your ideas in the graphic organizer below.

Story Title: <u>NEVER JUDGE A BOOK BY ITS COVER</u>

SETTING		
CHARACTER		
Main Heroes	Main Villains	Other Characters
PLOT		
Introduction	Conflict	Resolution
CONCLUSION		

C. Using the ideas in your story plan, write a draft of your story on the lines below.

_____

_____

_____

_____

_____

_____

_____

_____

_____

_____

_____

_____

_____

_____

_____

_____

To parents Ask your child to revise and improve the story above by removing unnecessary and repetitive words and using better nouns, verbs, adjectives and adverbs.

Vary Sentence Beginnings

Varying the way a sentence starts can add interest to your writing.

Study the four variations on this sentence: Kenji did his best karate routine.

You might start the sentence with:

- a prepositional phrase   *With pride*, Kenji did his best karate routine.

- a participial phrase   *Bowing to the teacher*, Kenji did his best karate routine.

- an adverb   *Modestly*, Kenji did his best karate routine.

- a subordinate clause   *Despite being nervous*, Kenji did his best karate routine.

A.   Write three different sentence beginnings for the following sentences.

1. _____, pigeons can be an urban nuisance.

2. _____, pigeons can be an urban nuisance.

3. _____, pigeons can be an urban nuisance.

4. _____, computers have changed the way people write.

5. _____, computers have changed the way people write.

6. _____, computers have changed the way people write.

B. Read the following passage. Change some of the sentence beginnings to add variety to the text.

The moth is very similar to a butterfly. The moth and the butterfly come from the same lineage. The moth, like the butterfly, grows from a caterpillar and forms a cocoon from which the moth emerges, fully grown. The moth is considered a pest as the caterpillar often eats agricultural plants or fabric and cloths. One species of moth however, is very valuable. The silkworm is farmed for the silk it uses to build its cocoon.

_____

_____

_____

_____

_____

_____

_____

_____

_____

_____

A Winning Beginning

A good opening sentence for a paragraph or essay can grab readers' attention and make them eager for more. Follow these three tips for starting out with a bang:

- Open with a strong sentence that uses bold, precise language.
- Present a challenge, ask a question, or offer a quotation to stir things up.
- Hint at what is to come.

A. Read these potential opening sentences. Each one could be improved. Think about how to make each one better and rewrite it for a winning beginning. Read the example given.

HINT: Avoid routine, ordinary openings, such as *There are* and *It is*.

1. There are many good reasons for eligible citizens to vote in the upcoming election.

   If eligible citizens fail to vote in Tuesday's election, they have only themselves to blame for an unwanted outcome.

2. The guided tours at the United States Mint are fascinating.

   _____

   _____

3. It takes training, ambition, and courage to be an astronaut.

   _____

   _____

To parents Ask your child to write a story or paragraph using an exaggeration as the beginning of the story. Suggest to your child to think big and over the top!

4. Singing in public can be very frightening for many people – even stars.

_____

_____

B. Look at the following topics. Write a good beginning to catch your reader's attention for each topic.

1. Your autobiography

_____

_____

_____

_____

2. An adventure story starting with the exploration of a run-down museum

_____

_____

_____

_____

_____

Classic Conflicts

In writing fiction stories, there are several types of **conflicts**:

- conflict with self: the character struggles internally
- conflict with others: the character has a problem with another character
- conflict with nature: the character(s) encounter a problem related to nature such as adverse weather conditions
- conflict with society: the character(s) face societal objections, is in a situation or has views that run contrary to mainstream society.

A.   Insert the heading to the correct conflict.

_____	_____	_____
Marc hacked into Jim's email and discovered Jim had lied to avoid the drug test by the sports department. Should he report it to the authorities?	Polly has been reprimanded by the discipline master for dying her hair pink. She finds this school rule about hair colour ridiculous.	Robinson Crusoe hung on to a plank and floated in the sea. There was no land in sight.
_____	_____	_____
"Put him into prison!" ordered Emperor Qing. "Jiang is the traitor, Your Majesty! You must believe me!" wailed Ming as the royal guards dragged him away.	"Stop crying now!" yelled Sally looking sadly at her scrawny son. They had not eaten for days. Where could she find food now?	"No jeans and sandals allowed into the concert hall, Sir," says the usher at the door. "What's wrong with jeans? They're long pants too!" yells Dad angrily.

B. Read the following setting and write three different conflict ideas for it.

"I should not have slapped him for playing truant," said Helen looking at the clock on the wall. Her son had not come home since the previous night. Helen tried but could not contact him on the handphone. The blizzard had grown stronger.

1. CONFLICT WITH SELF

_____

_____

_____

2. CONFLICT WITH SOCIETY

_____

_____

_____

3. CONFLICT WITH NATURE

_____

_____

_____

_____

Creating Suspense

Creating suspense keep your readers hooked on your story. It contains secrets or information that must be solved. Like detectives, your readers will be curious and use the clues to follow your story. You can create suspense by having an intriguing beginning, setting, suspicious characters, clues, plot or twists.

A. How does the writer create suspense in the following story? Read the story, then answer the following questions.

An hour in the cave felt like eternity. Don and Jack could not wait to find the royal pearl in the inner chamber and leave. They must get it before it landed in the hands of wicked Wizard Ale. In total darkness, the two boys groped the icy walls stumbling deeper and deeper into the cave. Water began filling up to their knees. The flapping sound grew louder. Suddenly, Don waved his hands wildly. "Something just grabbed my shoulders!" screamed Don. "Stay calm!" said Jack trying to reach Don but it was just futile. Don kept yelling and splashing water about. All of a sudden, there was silence. "Are you alright, Don?" asked Jack. All he could hear was the dripping of water.

1. How do the descriptions engage the reader? What kinds of details does the writer provide?

_____

_____

_____

2. What information does the writer omit to create suspense?

_____

_____

_____

B. Imagine you are writing a paragraph for a crime story. Use the information to create suspense for the following scene.

Setting

- Place: Apartment
- Timing: Midnight
- Set-up for suspense: The residents had been warned about the recent robberies in the block. A drawing of the suspects was pinned on the board beside the elevator. Kelly had just returned home from work. She found the drawing familiar; somewhat like her new next-door neighbors. But she shrugged off the idea because they were newly-weds and had gone overseas for their honeymoon.

Create a scene in Kelly's home where something odd happened and Kelly suspected that she was being robbed. Remember to omit some details so your readers would be curious to read on.

_____

_____

_____

_____

_____

_____

_____

_____

A Moving Plot

A **moving plot** is an essential part of a good story. A moving plot includes:

- an attractive introduction to set up your story
- a elaborate middle with various twists and turns building up to a climax
- a satisfying ending that either makes your reader happy, sad, surprised or have learned something from your story.

A. Jot down points for a story. Choose from the given topics. Use the questions in the second column to help you.

- A Murder in Gilman Hall
- Treasure Hunting
- The Chase

Introduction	INTRODUCTION • Introduce your characters • Set up for conflict / problem (who, what where, when, why)
Middle	MIDDLE • Rising action: What are the events that lead to the climax? • Climax: What is the turning point at which the main character decides on how to resolve the problem? • Falling action: What are the events after the climax?
Conclusion	ENDING • Close with a happy, sad, serious or surprising resolution to the conflict / problem

B. Now write your story below. Remember that sometimes, we can omit important information initially to create suspense and help move the plot forward.

_____

_____

_____

_____

_____

_____

_____

_____

_____

_____

_____

_____

_____

_____

Come to a Memorable Close

A good piece of writing should come to a logical conclusion. It shouldn't just stop! Follow these three tips for coming to a **memorable close**:

- Revisit the main idea in another way.
- Present a decision or state a plan of action.
- End with a bang—ask a question, cite a quotation, give an opinion.

A. Read the following endings. Underline the more memorable ending.

Tina sat down and thought about everything that had passed. They finally found out who stole the shoes. She knew that Gavin stole them because he wanted his sister to have a pair of shoes but their family couldn't afford it. In the end, she decided to give his sister the pair of shoes and she felt good about it.

Tina pondered over how fortunate she is. When she learned why Gavin stole the shoes, she was struck that there were families that couldn't afford a simple pair of shoes. She decided to give Gavin's sister the pair of shoes and the feeling of giving was amazing!

B. Why did you find the ending you underlined more memorable?

_____

_____

_____

C. Can you improve on the endings given? Write a new ending using the points above.

_____

_____

_____

_____

_____

D. Read these weak closing sentences for essays on the given topic. Think
    about how to make each one better. Rewrite it to suggest a memorable
    closing for the essay.

    HINT: People remember the last thing they read—so make it count!

1. [*Essay on responsibility*] Never put off doing your part for your community.

    _____

    _____

2. [*Anecdote about whales*] That's my story about whales. _____

    _____

3. [*Report on clouds*] I don't think I'll ever look at clouds the same way again.

    _____

    _____

4. [*Movie review*] Fans of scary science fiction will love this film. _____

    _____

Let's Exaggerate

> When you exaggerate, you stretch the truth. **Exaggeration** makes things seem much bigger or smaller. It can make things seem much better or worse.
>
> *Okay:*   Cathy takes a long time to get ready for school.
>
> *Better:*   Cathy takes forever to decide what to wear for the party.

A.   Fill in each blank with a suitable exaggeration.

1.   You are the best friend in _____.

2.   "Is dinner ready, Mum? I'm so hungry I could eat _____!" yelled Chris.

3.   This suitcase weighs _____! What did you put in there to make it so heavy?

4.   This is the coldest winter I've ever experienced. I'm freezing _____.

5.   She has walked this route _____ but she still gets lost!

6.   We could smell Uncle Tim's fried chicken from _____.

7.   Megan walks so slowly; _____ could faster than her!

8.   The music was so loud it could _____.

9.   That piece of machinery is so old and useless, it might as well be

     _____.

10.   He lost so much weight that he is _____.

B. Imagine a new neighbor has just moved in next door to you. Something is special about the child. Draw a picture of the child in the box. Then write a ten-line poem about his appearance and interesting behavior. Be sure to exaggerate your descriptions.

IMAGE	POEM

Transitions 1

Transitions link ideas to make them easier to follow and relationships more clear. Here are four types of transitions with "signal words" for each:

Cause/Effect — *as a result, because, due to, since, so that, then, therefore, thus, without*

Chronology — *after, before, during, finally, meanwhile, next, once, previously, suddenly*

Contrast — *although, but, however, on the other hand, rather, similarly, still, yet*

Conclusion — *at last, finally, for that reason, in conclusion, in summary, since, so, therefore*

A.   Complete each sentence with the best transition word from the above list.

1.   _____ the storm, a rainbow appeared in the clear blue sky.

2.   _____ the swelling, I had to cushion my feet and rest in bed for a week.

3.   James moved. _____ he could see the target better.

4.   _____ that air has weight, Mr Bobby inflated a balloon and let it go from the top of the school.

5.   "Mayday Mayday, from Town Jakerson!" cried Thomson looking at the

      iceberg, _____ there was no reply.

6.   For the experiment, we have to find a firefly for light. _____ that, we have to keep it alive for a week.

7.   Like a sack, Tim lay at a corner _____ he was bruised all over.

8.   _____ on Kelly's insistence, I bought the cowboy hat.

B. Complete the story with the correct transition words from the box.

so	besides	hence	since	before
whereas	as	overall	eventually	

Finally, I reached the ground. This was a strange new world! The sand felt

soft like flour. Everything was quiet. All I could hear was my own breathing.

I had not felt such peace (1) _____ I lost Dad two year ago. The

water was clear and comforting, (2) _____ I relaxed and let go of

the rope. I floated around and paddled out to join Randy and the rest. This

was my first time (3) _____ Randy had been to so many expeditions

like this. He had asked me to come (4) _____ but I was just too

scared. (5) _____, I could not swim then. Now, it was a different

story. The corals danced around (6) _____ the clown fish played

hide-and-seek with me. (7) _____, I gave up and looked for

Randy. He signalled excitedly. (8) _____, I followed up. And there,

among the rocks, was my favorite animal. I lay my hand on its shell gently.

A green ring surrounded my palm. I would have kept my hand there forever

if it had not wriggled and disappeared away. (9) _____, it had

been the one of the most memorable trips of my life.

Transitions 2

A. Complete the list with the correct transition words from the box.

In fact	Eventually	Moreover	With this in mind
Hence	Consequently	To illustrate	On the other hand
Since	Overall	In order to	Subsequently
Due to	Nevertheless	Therefore	To demonstrate

TO ADD INFORMATION	
TO INDICATE PURPOSE	
TO INDICATE TIME FRAME / SHIFT	
TO COMPARE OR CONTRAST	
TO STATE AN EXAMPLE	
TO CONCLUDE	
TO GIVE A CAUSE / REASON	
TO SHOW A RESULT / EFFECT	

B. Complete the rest of the sentence after the transition so that the ideas go together sensibly.

HINT: Think of transitions as signposts in the form of word clues.

1. Fierce winds battered the town for several hours. As a result, _____

_____

2. Dad prepared the 18-pound turkey for oyster stuffing. Meanwhile, I _____

_____

_____

C. Consider the meaning of each transition. Then write a sentence that could come before it.

1. _____.

Therefore, we had no choice but to postpone the picnic.

2. _____.

Previously, such items could be made only by hand.

D. Write a pair of sentences connected with a different kind of transition.

1. [Cause/Effect] _____

_____

2. [Chronology] _____

_____

Writing a Review

A **review** is an evaluation of a piece of work. This could be a movie, a song, artwork or piece of writing. It offers an opinion of the piece of work. Sometimes it requires the writer to be familiar with the topic.

A.   Read the following details and complete them with the correct headings.

A Review on a _____	A Review on a _____
• Largest screening complex in town	• Huge covered area
• Twenty air-conditioned theatres	• Sponge pool for toddlers 2-4 years old; sponge balls too small for toddlers; dangerous; may swallow them
• The only place that screens foreign art films	
• Large screens and surround sound systems	• Slides and swings for kids 3-8 years old
• Comfortable seats with drink-holders	• Multi-sensory corner with lights and music; suitable therapy for special needs kids, but too small; only two kids at a time
• 10% discount on tickets for students and the elderly	
• Stores selling film merchandise; artistes' autograph	• Entrance fee of $15 per kid, rather expensive
• Regular sessions	• Overall, an interesting place that would be better with cheaper entrance fee and safer equipment; will not recommend for parents to bring kids there.
• A good leisure place for family and friends	

B.   Imagine you are a journalist for a lifestyle magazine and have to write a review of a new restaurant in town. Complete the graphic organizer.

Review on: _____

Location / History:	Environment:
Staff / Service:	**Choice and Quality of Food:**
Price and Value:	**Other Remarks:**

Research and Report

Writing a **report** requires the writer to research on facts about the topic, organize them and present a neutral point of view.

A.   Read the following topics and put them under the correct headings.

Who is JK Rowling?

How does a camera work?

How is a tsunami created?

How is floor ball different from other types of hockey?

How do Japanese celebrate the New Year?

Why do soft-shell crabs have soft-shells?

Why are there so many volcanoes in Indonesia?

What happened to Singapore during the Second World War?

People:	
Culture:	
History:	
Geography:	
Science:	
Sport:	
Animal:	
Nature:	

B. Imagine you are a journalist for a kids magazine. Write a nonfiction report on people, science or animals. Complete the graphic organizer before you begin your draft.

Topic Question	
Target Readers	
Facts and Examples	

C. Write a draft of the report.

_____

_____

_____

_____

_____

_____

Letter for a Cause

A **persuasive essay** is used to convince others of an idea or opinion your have. Persuasive essays can come in many forms including letters or editorials.

A. Use the following table to plan your persuasive letter. Complete the table with the correct heading from the box.

OPINION STATEMENT REASONS & DETAILS	EXPECTED REBUTTALS WRITER'S RESPONSE	TARGET READER PURPOSE OF LETTER

	• Park Ranger • Director at a TV station
	• To request park ranger to have law against fishing in the park • To request TV station to stop screening violent movies on their channels
	• Parks should disallow people from fishing in the pond. • No more violent movies on TV
	• Fishing will disrupt the animal and plant eco-systems. • Children may become violent from imitating the violence watched in the movies.
	• Fishing is good leisure activity. My response: Over-fishing reduces the population of fishes which may become extinct. • Switch channel if you do not want to watch them. My response: Many families watch TV together. Having wholesome content will allow all to enjoy family time together.

B. Imagine you are writing a letter to the park ranger or to a producer at a TV station. Use the points in Part A to write your letter.

_____

_____
_____

_____

_____

_____

_____

_____

_____

_____

_____

_____

_____

Solving a Problem

> Writing a **problem-solution essay** is a good way of convincing others to agree and take an action you recommend.

A. Imagine you are writing an essay to your local newspaper to highlight a problem on the dangers of night cycling. Plan your essay with the table below.

State the problem • What is the problem?	
Suggest solution • What are the possible solutions for each problem?	
Support solution with details • For each solution, add details of what can be done.	
Highlight potential problem with solution • Are there problems with the solution? • Highlight what needs to be done for your solutions to work.	

B.   Then write your essay on the lines below.

_____

_____

_____

_____

_____

_____

_____

_____

_____

_____

_____

_____

_____

_____

_____

_____

To parents   Get your child to review the solutions presented and think of counter-solutions.

Stay on Track

It is important to **stay focused on the main points** in your writing. Writing off the topic will confuse your readers.

A. Read the following paragraphs and circle the points that are not relevant or may confuse the readers.

Paragraph 1

Kite-Flying for All

Children are not the only ones who can fly kites. Kite-flying should be encouraged in schools and families. It takes good weather to fly kites. It is a good leisure activity for parents with their children. In some countries like United Kingdom and Malaysia, there are kite festivals where experts fly gigantic kites they have designed themselves. These experts are mostly adult amateur kite-fliers. Some of them play music too.

Paragraph 2

A Nightmare on Matt Street

11pm. The street is deserted. The garbage bins are full. The trees ruffled noisily above me. I quickened my steps. "Keep walking. Don't look back," I mutter repeatedly. Suddenly, I felt a pat on my shoulders. I froze. The ground was wet from the afternoon rain. Slowly, I turned. My hair was messy from the running.

B. Imagine you are writing a brochure about a famous place for your local tourism board. Use the graphic organizer to plan your brochure.

Place of Interest	
Attractions at the Place	
Getting There	
Costs	

C. Write your brochure below.

_____

_____

_____

_____

_____

Unity in Paragraphs

A paragraph has unity when all its sentences relate to its main idea. Even a sentence that may be interesting and well-written just does not belong if it fails to support the main idea.

A. Read each paragraph. Each has a sentence that states its main idea. Underline it. Next, cross out the sentence that does not belong. Then explain your decision.

HINT: Imagine a paragraph as a team with one goal. Take out any ideas that are off-topic.

1. Tutankhamun ruled Egypt for less than ten years starting in about 1334 BC. He reigned in the eighteenth dynasty of the New Kingdom. Although historians don't think that King Tut was an influential monarch in his day, a rare find in 1922 made him a celebrity. That was when archaeologist Howard Carter discovered the hidden tomb of the so-called Boy King. Carter died in 1939 at home in England. His findings were so spectacular that the whole world soon learned about King Tut and eagerly sought information about the treasures of his tomb.

_____

_____

2. Ancient Egypt was a land of many perils. Scorching heat was a fact of life. Deadly animals, such as lions, crocodiles, snakes, and scorpions, prowled regularly. The Nile River provided water, transportation and fertile soil. There were floods, dust storms, and earthquakes. Little was known about the invisible causes of most diseases. So Egyptian healers gathered as much knowledge as they could about treating injury and disease. They mixed science with mythology and religion to come up with effective treatments for the body.

_____

_____

B. Read the following points to support the topic: Breakfast is Important

- Kids need breakfast more than adults do.

- Provides the body with energy resulting in improved efficiency.

- Adults should prepare breakfast the night before to save time.

- Results in healthier life and better immunity levels.

- Studies show that those who skip breakfast take longer to do a task and fall sick more often.

- Skipping breakfast is linked to obesity and makes controlling weight gain difficult.

- Those who skip breakfast tend to eat more at the next meal or take more snacks.

- Eating well should be accompanied by regular exercise.

Write two paragraphs for the topic below. Use only the relevant points above to write your paragraphs. Remember that each paragraph should have a topic sentence and supporting details.

_____

_____

_____

_____

_____

_____

_____

Elaborating in Different Ways

There are various ways to elaborate and add details to a text.

A. Read the following text. Change some of the dull words and choose more precise nouns, adjectives, adverbs or verbs to improve the text. Cross out the words you want to replace and write the revised words above them.

It was dark and the streets were not well-lit. Police Inspector Don was out

patrolling with his new partner, Paul. This was their first night out together.

It was also Paul's first day in the new department.

"Be alert. This is the most dangerous street," said Don. Paul held his pistol

tightly and scanned the blocks around them. All the shops were closed

except for the gaming arcade at the far corner. Trendily dressed teens

streamed in and out of the narrow door. "Be careful of those young punks,"

said Don. Paul said. "Those noisy kids? They are just playing, Don," said

Paul watching the boys laughing and pushing one another.

All of a sudden, a scream came from the crowd as a skinny boy fell

holding his stomach in pain.

B. Now improve the text further by doing the following:
- Add descriptive details to increase suspense
- Reduce unnecessary and repetitive words
- Vary sentence structure and length

Write your revised text below.

_____

_____

_____

_____

_____

_____

_____

_____

_____

_____

_____

_____

Elaborating without Repeating

Sometimes writers repeat their points when adding details by saying the same thing in a different way. This can make the writing dull and tedious to read. It is important to provide details while keeping your writing succinct.

A. Rewrite the following descriptions. Remove the repetitious information or phrases. You may want to change the structure of sentences as well.

1. Dad was finally coming home. He has been away for almost ten years. It has been so long that I wondered if I would still recognize him. He was stuck in a foreign land, held captive by rebels for many years. The rebels were recently defeated and the captives were finally released.

    _____

    _____

    _____

    _____

    _____

    _____

2. When I saw him, my heart stopped. I didn't know what to say and I was speechless. What do you say to someone who has been away for ten years? He looked thin, emaciated and weary. It was as if the spark had gone out of him and all that was left was an outer shell. Dad wasn't the only one. All the captives who were freed looked like that.

    _____

    _____

_____

_____

_____

_____

B.   Elaborate on the following description. Keep your writing succinct. Add new details to your description instead of repeating the ones you wrote.

First, we saw the crowds at the beach run towards us in panic. Then, we saw the huge waves that had swelled over the ocean and were about to crash onto the shore. I was rooted to the spot both in fear and awe. Then I felt someone grab me and run.

1.   What else were the crowds doing besides running? Describe the scene of panic.

_____

_____

_____

2.   What other details can you add about the waves?

_____

_____

_____

3.   What else did the narrator of the story do?

_____

_____

_____

Elaboration Editor

You have learned many techniques for elaboration. Now is your chance to put these ideas to use.

Edit and revise the following draft of a movie review. Write the improved review on separate paper.

HINT: Jot down ideas on the draft. Make any changes that will improve the piece.

The movie was supposed to be a comedy. But it wasn't as funny as I

thought it would be. The previews were okay. They made me think it would be

a laugh riot, and I was looking forward to seeing it with my friends on

opening day. But it was just stupid. The only funny scene was the one I saw in

the previews. The rest of the movie stank. Even the opening was dull.

The main character is a shy and nervous man who wants to be a

standup comic. He isn't very good with people, but he thinks he is funny.

He thinks he will get popular if he can be a famous comedian. His friends

are mostly into serious topics. He reads books about how to tell jokes

and watches videos of comics to get ideas. But he always gets it wrong.

He is weird. He yells for no good reason. His jokes are obnoxious. And not

funny. He makes a deal with the owner of a comedy club to...

I won't say what happens. I think you should form your own

opinion. The star is very famous. You might expect his movies to be

good. It also has a soundtrack by many popular musicians. The title

song is by my favorite band, Second to None. Second to None writes

great songs, has a great lead singer, and has at least four (maybe five

or six) great albums.

Anyway, even great music can't save a stupid movie. This film

was just too mean. I didn't like the main character. I didn't care what

happened to him. And his sense of humor is so terrible.

Test Prep Tips

Some standardized tests ask you to write a story, an anecdote, a letter, or other kind of narrative piece. In addition, they may require you to complete the piece of writing within a time limit and without teacher assistance or reference materials. By applying the elaboration techniques you have learned, you should experience greater success in such formal assessment situations.

Here are some tried and true test-taking techniques.

Before you write

* Read all directions carefully and completely.
* Give yourself a few moments to think and plan.
* Narrow your focus.
* Think about your audience.
* Make notes, or use graphic organizers to get started.
* Group ideas that go together. Cross out ideas you do not need.
* Make an organizational plan of how to present your ideas.

Looking back, ask yourself

* Did I make my point clearly and effectively?
* Did I stick to my topic?
* Did I support main ideas with adequate details?
* Do my paragraphs have unity?
* Did I write a winning beginning and a memorable ending?
* Is there anything else I ought to add or delete?
* Did I fix errors in spelling, capitalization, and punctuation?
* Is my handwriting legible?

Common Editing Symbols

Symbol	Meaning	Example
⟋	Delete (Take it away forever!)	a ~~tiny~~ kitten
— ⌃	Delete and change to something else	sleep all ~~day~~ ⌃night
¶	Begin a new paragraph	¶ It was a dark and stormy night.
ⓛⓒ	Lowercase that capital letter	ⓛⓒ A /Horse's mane
ⓒⓐⓟ ≡	Capitalize that lowercase letter	ⓒⓐⓟ in Santa Fe, New mexico≡
⌃	Insert comma	Cheyenne⌃Wyoming
⌄⌄ ⌄⌄	Insert quotation marks	Carlos asked, ⌄⌄How are you?⌄⌄
⊙ ⌃	Insert period	An ant ambled about ⊙⌃
? ⌃	Insert question mark	Where is Copenhagen?⌃
∼	Transpose (or trade positions)	A cat slipped on the floor waxed .
ⓢⓟ	Check the spelling	ⓢⓟ ⟨wether⟩

124

Self-Prompting Hints

Read your writing out loud. Listen to yourself.

- ❏   Does it sound right?
- ❏   Where could I use a better word?
- ❏   Did I leave out a word or idea?
- ❏   Did I overuse any words?
- ❏   Do I need more supporting details or examples?
- ❏   Could I write an idea more completely?
- ❏   Do my sentences flow smoothly?
- ❏   Does my writing sound interesting?
- ❏   Does every sentence in a paragraph support the main idea?
- ❏   Is there anything that doesn't belong?

Notice the rise and fall of your voice.

- ❏   If I *stop*, is there a <u>period</u>?
- ❏   If I *pause*, is there a <u>comma</u>?
- ❏   If my voice *rises*, is there a <u>question mark</u>?
- ❏   Do any of my sentences need an <u>exclamation point</u> for *emphasis*?

Read your whole piece.

- ❏   Will it grab and hold a reader's attention?
- ❏   Does the piece paint a picture?
- ❏   Will readers be able to tell the characters apart?
- ❏   Did I vary sentence lengths and types?
- ❏   Did I vary sentence structures and beginnings?
- ❏   Are there parts I can improve by adding figurative language?
- ❏   Is my point of view or opinion clear?
- ❏   Does the dialogue sound like words people really say?
- ❏   Does it have a memorable ending?

Answers

Pages 6–7
A. 1. Betsy is baking a cake in the kitchen.
   2. That dog charged at me and barked ferociously.
   3. Fries are made from potatoes.
   4. The guard locks up the school at 8pm every night.
B. *These are suggested answers.*
   1. bowl 2. sheep 3. tents 4. guitar
C. 1. houses 2. restaurant 3. dive 4. sea
   5. boat 6. waves 7. fear 8. photos

Pages 8–9 *Accept reasonable answers.*

Pages 10–11
A. 1. knowledge
   2. maturity
   3. imagination
   4. strength
   5. sorrow / regret
   6. acceptance
   7. disappointment
   8. independence
   9. enjoyment
   10. humility
B. 1. maturity   2. knowledge   3. disappointment
   4. independence 5. imagination
C. 1. poverty 2. loyalty 3. starvation
   4. pride 5. bravery
D. *Accept reasonable answers.*

Pages 12–13 *Accept reasonable answers.*

Pages 14–15
A. longer   longest
   noisier   noisiest
   funnier   funniest
   more majestic   most majestic
   more complicated   most complicated
   more beautiful   most beautiful
   better   best
   worse   worst
   more   most
B. 1. better   2. more diligent, more intelligent
   3. most good-looking 4. funniest 5. messiest
C. *These are suggested answers.*
   1. old 2. long 3. busiest 4. worst
   5. best 6. friendliest
D. *Accept reasonable answers.*

Pages 16–17
A. *Accept reasonable answers.*
B. *These are suggested answers.*
   1. examined, checked   5. rested
   2. marched, went up   6. failed, neglected
   3. exclaimed, cried   7. pushed, thrust
   4. marched, stomped   8. broke, barged
C. *Accept reasonable answers.*

Pages 18–19
A. *These are suggested answers.*
   1. screamed 2. galloped 3. screeched 4. gobbled
B and C. *Accept reasonable answers.*

Pages 20–21
A. 1. suitcase 2. steel   3. cold
   4. hurled 5. scratches
   1. fly   2. wings 3. fracture / wound
   4. nest   5. winter
B. *Accept reasonable answers.*

Pages 22–23
A. *These are suggested answers.*
   1. I play computer games daily.
   2. I always / usually go to the nearest ice-cream shop
      with friends.
   3. I spend only a few hours watching TV each day.
   4. I would best like to go to the restaurant at the town
      square for a yummy meal.
   5. I can't say as I seldom fail a test.
B. *These are suggested answers.*
   1. gently   2. quickly   3. excitedly 4. brightly
   5. busily   6. quietly   7. carefully 8. fondly
   9. eagerly 10. frantically

Pages 24–29 *Accept reasonable answers.*

Pages 30–31
A. 1. villain – hero
   2. hilarious – boring
   3. elderly – children
   4. laughed – sobbed
   5. dark – bright
   6. give – receive
B. *Accept reasonable answers.*

Pages 32–33

A. *These are suggested answers.*
1. unsafe   2. raise / increase
3. professional 4. graceful
5. bottom   6. reward
7. sensible   8. spirit
9. last   10. an adult

B. 1. a safe investment
2. see you at the summit
3. the spirit was overwhelming
4. the most sensible reply
5. As a reward

C and D. *Accept reasonable answers.*

Pages 34–41 *Accept reasonable answers.*

Pages 42–43

A. 1. because Wolly forgot to turn off the tap (cause)
2. when the celebrity soccer player arrived (cause)
3. Jane was scolded (effect)
4. the mountaineers could see the peak (effect)
5. after a long day out at sea (cause)
6. and you will get a free mug (effect)
7. having run 5km round the field (cause)
8. the sniper aimed at the target (effect)

B. These are suggested answers.
1. As it was snowing outside, the school was closed for the day.
2. She missed the bus because she woke up late.
3. Keane left the report he has been working on at home as he left in a hurry.
4. Because he failed to pay his taxes, he had to pay a hefty fine.
5. The manager was promoted when he came with a way to save money for the company.

C. *Accept reasonable answers.*

Pages 44–45

A. *Accept reasonable answers.*
B. 1. b 2. b 3. c
C and D. *Accept reasonable answers.*

Pages 46–47

A. 1. as happy as a lark
2. like a mad dog
3. like a bull
4. As quick as lightning
5. like a cheese bun
6. as cool as a cucumber
7. like a baby
8. as stubborn as a donkey

B. *Accept reasonable answers.*
C. 1. as silk
2. like a giraffe
3. as slow as a snail
4. as proud as a peacock
5. as timid as a rabbit
6. as solid as a rock
7. as plain as day
8. as stubborn as a mule

Pages 48–49

A. 1. reading = heaven; meaning: reading on a rainy day is very enjoyable
2. I = volcano; meaning: I got very angry
3. Small boy = prince; meaning: the boy was very pampered
4. Heart = stone; meaning: hard-hearted
5. She = walking dictionary; meaning: she has a very large vocabulary

B. 1. ostrich 2. rag doll 3. giant 4. fool
5. hero   6. bulls   7. fox   8. mouse

Pages 50–53 *Accept reasonable answers.*

Pages 54–55

A. 1. like vultures   2. as smooth as glass
3. as hot as an oven   4. like soldiers
5. hell   6. a chicken
7. a bank   8. a tortoise
9. flashed   10. danced beautifully

B and C. *Accept reasonable answers.*

Pages 56–57

A. A2, B2, C2, D2
B. 1. (b) 2. (a) 3.(b)
C. *Accept reasonable answers.*
D. 1. burst 2. black 3. ploughed/broke
4. thick 5. screamed

Pages 58–59 *Accept reasonable answers.*

Pages 60–61

A. Sadness – Slumping in the seat; Head in her hands; Looking down
Anger – Crossing of arms
Happy – Skipping across the hall
Nervous – Crossing fingers; Pacing up and down; Looking down
Victorious – Punching the air
B. *Accept reasonable answers.*

Pages 62–63

A. 1. e 2. i 3. j 4. a 5. c
   6. h 7. b 8. f 9. d 10. g

B. 1. did her hair
   2. went blind
   3. excruciating pain
   4. broke her promise
   5. completely satisfied
   6. take a look
   7. broke the record
   8. made a mess
   9. save time
   10. came into view
   11. burst into tears
   12. caught his attention

Pages 64–65

A. HAVE: have a good time, have lunch
   DO: do business, the housework
   MAKE: make a difference, make trouble
   TAKE: take a seat, take an exam
   BREAK: break the law, break a habit
   CATCH: catch a cold, catch fire
   PAY: pay a compliment, pay interest, pay the price
   SAVE: save space, save someone's life
   KEEP: keep a diary, keep calm
   GO: go astray, go abroad
   COME: come early, come clean
   GET: get a job

B. *Accept reasonable answers.*

C. 1. found a job
   2. have a good time
   3. grew dark
   4. take a break
   5. have my fill
   6. running out of cash

Pages 66–69 *Accept reasonable answers.*

Pages 70–71

A. These are suggested answers.
   1. Active / Harry was turned into a hawk by Wizard Warner with the wave of his wand.
   2. Passive / The hurricane swept all the houses into the sea.
   3. Passive / Some people consider the durian fruit a delicacy.
   4. Active / The hooligans were warned by the police to stop extorting money from the boys.
   5. Active / Many children in the village were killed by the drought.

B and C. *Accept reasonable answers.*

Pages 72–73

A. 1. Simple 2. Complex 3. Compound
   4. Complex 5. Simple 6. Compound

B. *Accept reasonable answers.*

Pages 74–80 *Accept reasonable answers.*

Pages 81–82

A. Positive: optimistic, cheerful, encouraging, comforting
   Neutral: quiet, relaxed
   Negative: mournful, skeptical, irritated, aloof, bored, intimidating

B. *Accept reasonable answers.*

Pages 83–100

Accept reasonable answers.

Pages 101–102

A. *Accept reasonable answers.*

B. 1. since 2. so 3. whereas
   4. before 5. Besides 6. as
   7. Eventually 8. Hence 9. Overall

Pages 103–106

Accept reasonable answers.

Pages 107–108

A. People: Who is JK Rowling?
   Culture: How do Japanese celebrate the New Year?
   History: What happened to Singapore during the Second World War?
   Geography: Why are there so many volcanoes in Indonesia?
   Science: How does a camera work?
   Sport: How is floor ball different from other types of hockey?
   Animal: Why do soft-shell crabs have soft shells?
   Nature: How is a tsunami created?

B and C. *Accept reasonable answers.*

Page 109

A. Target Reader, Purpose of Letter, Opinion Statement, Reasons and Details, Expected Rebuttals and Writer's Response

Pages 110–123

Accept reasonable answers.